Short-eared Owl

Those Outrageous Owls

Laura Wyatt

Illustrations by Steve Weaver

Pineapple Press, Inc.

Sarasota, Florida

Inquiries should be addressed to:
Pineapple Press, Inc.
P.O. Box 3889
Sarasota, Florida 34230
www.pineapplepress.com

Library of Congress Cataloging-in-Publication Data

Wyatt, Laura, 1977-
Those outrageous owls / Laura Wyatt.-- 1st ed.
p. cm.
Includes bibliographical references (p.) and index.
ISBN-13: 978-1-56164-365-3 (hardback : alk. paper)
ISBN-10: 1-56164-365-3 (hardback : alk. paper)
ISBN-13: 978-1-56164-366-0 (paper back : alk. paper)
ISBN-10: 1-56164-366-1 (pbk. : alk. paper)
1. Owls--Juvenile literature. I. Title.
QL696.S83W93 2006
598.9'7--dc22

2006004954

First Edition
Hb 10 9 8 7 6 5 4 3 2 1
Pb 10 9 8 7 6 5 4 3 2

Design by Steve Weaver
Printed in the United States of America

To Michael

Contents

Barred Owl

What is an owl?

Owls are in a group of birds called raptors or birds of prey. That means they eat meat, catching their live food (prey) with their talons (feet with claws). Birds of prey include other birds like hawks and eagles. Owls have a hooked beak and very good vision and hearing. Most owls are awake during twilight and nighttime.

Great Horned Owlets

Who's the boy and who's the girl?

Female owls are larger. This helps a mother owl protect her young and the nest. Male owls are smaller so they can hunt more easily. Male owls provide most of the food for the females and their young.

Screech Owl

Why do owls have such funny feet?

An owl's feet (called talons) are strong with sharp claws. Owls use their feet to catch their food. Once an owl grasps its food, its powerful talons lock down tightly. Owls have two toes facing forward and two toes backwards. This helps them climb trees.

Barred Owl

What do owls eat?

Smaller owls eat insects, frogs, lizards, and small rodents. Larger owls eat rodents, like mice and rats, and other small mammals. They cannot digest the bones, feathers, or fur. The next day they will cough up a pellet. This pellet is filled with the bones, feathers, and fur from the food they ate the night before.

Barred Owl

How do owls hunt?

Owls use their eyes and ears to find food. Most owls hunt at night and can see well in the dark. They fly in silently and use their talons to catch their prey.

Barn Owl

How do owls fly so quietly?

Owls have very soft feathers. At the end of each feather are even softer feathers called barbs. These barbs soften the sound of the air rushing over the wings, making an owl almost silent when it flies. This means that the owl can better hear its prey, and it also means the prey cannot hear the owl coming.

Barred Owl

How do owls hear?

Owls' ears are different from ours. One ear is higher than the other. When an owl hears a noise in both ears at the same time, it knows that it is looking right at its target. Owls' ears are so sensitive that they can find their prey in complete darkness.

Barred Owl

Why do owls have such round faces?

Owls have a facial disk. This facial disk acts like a "radar dish." It helps gather and guide sound to the ears. The owl can even change the shape of the disk, using special face muscles, so that it can guide the sound even better.

Great Horned Owl

Why are owls' eyes so big and why do they look so wise?

Owls use their big eyes to help them see in the dark. An owl's eyes are so large that they take up almost the entire skull. If we had eyes like owls, they would be as large as grapefruits! Owls' eyes face forward like ours, so they can look at an object with both eyes at the same time. Also, an owl cannot turn its eyes. An owl looks wise because its eyes are very big, face forward, and look straight ahead.

Screech Owl

Can an owl turn its head all the way around?

An owl makes up for not being able to turn its eyes by being able to turn its head almost all the way around and almost upside-down. An owl can do this because it has special muscles and lots of little bones in its neck.

Great Horned Owl

Why do owls hoot?

Not all owls hoot. Some owls, like the Screech Owls and Barn Owls, make a screech or scream. Owls hoot to locate each other. Some owls hoot for their mates. Some hoots are warnings to other owls to stay away.

Burrowing Owl

When do owls sleep?

Almost all owls are up at night and sleep during the day. These owls are called nocturnal. This is why people who stay up late are called "night owls." However, some owls, like the wide-awake Burrowing Owl in this photo, can be seen during the day. These owls are called diurnal.

Screech Owl

Why do owls look the way they do?

Owls are colored to blend in with their environment. This is called camouflage. It's just like soldiers who wear camouflage clothing so they won't be seen by the enemy. A lot of owls have feathers that look like a tree bark or leaves. Snowy owls are white to blend in with snow.

Screech Owl

What kind of nest does an owl use?

Most owls nest in old dead trees. Some owls, like the Great Horned Owl, steal other birds' nests. Barn Owls use old barns and abandoned buildings as nest sites. Burrowing Owls dig holes in the ground to lay their eggs.

Burrowing Owl Eggs

How many eggs does an owl lay?

Most owls lay 3 or 4 eggs. The female lays one egg every day or two. The eggs are white. Since the nest is hidden, the eggs do not need to look dark like the nest to keep them safe from other animals who might eat them. Owlets will start to hatch in about 30 days. The owlets hatch on different days, causing them to be different sizes.

Barn Owl

What does an owlet look like?

When an owlet is born it looks like a cotton ball. The owlets have soft, fluffy feathers. These downy feathers help keep the baby owls warm. The father owl delivers food to the owlets as often as 10 times a day.

Great Horned Owl

When is an owl all grown up?

Some owls are fully feathered and grown at one month of age. Larger owls may take up to three months to get all their feathers. Some owls will live with their parents for almost a whole year before they go out on their own.

Great Horned Owl

Why do horned owls have horns?

Some owls look like they have horns. It was once thought that the horns were ears, but they are feathers. These horns help an owl blend in and make it invisible against a tree. The horns also show what kind of mood the owl is in.

Great Gray Owl

Elf Owl

How many kinds of owls are there?

There are more than 200 species of owls worldwide. Owls live on every continent except Antarctica.

Some of the largest owls in the world include the Great Gray Owl and the Eurasian Eagle Owl. The smallest owls in the world are the Elf Owl and Least Pygmy Owl. Owls can be found almost everywhere. They can live in thick forests, oak hammocks, open fields, and even in your own backyard (unless you live in Antarctica, of course).

Short-eared Owl

Why are owls important to us?

Owls help control insects and rodents. An adult owl can eat 3,000 rodents in one year. This saves us millions of dollars and prevents us from using harmful chemicals. We can help owls by leaving dead trees standing. This is their favorite nesting spot.

Make a Bag Owl

You will need:

Brown bag

Newspaper

Glue or tape

1 big round leaf

2 small round leaves

2 large pointed leaves

3 medium-size pointed leaves

2 large leaves

(Note: all leaves should be dry)

2 sticks

Stuff your bag with wadded newspaper. Fold up the bottom and glue or tape it shut. Attach the large leaf for the owl's face. Attach the two small round leaves for eyes. Attach one pointed leaf for the nose. Attach the other two pointed leaves for horns. Attach two large leaves on the sides for wings. Attach two sticks for feet.

Make a whole family tree of owls. Use different size bags and leaves to create Mom, Dad, and baby owlets.

Make a Heart Owl

You will need:

Colored paper

Scissors

Glue

Trace the hearts on colored paper and create your own Heart Owl.

Glossary

barb – a very soft projection at the end of a feather

bird of prey – a bird that gets its food by hunting animals (also called a raptor)

camouflage – natural coloring or form that enables an animal to blend in with its surroundings

diurnal – most active during the daytime

downy – covered with fine, soft, fluffy feathers

nocturnal – most active at night

owl – a bird of prey that is usually nocturnal and has large eyes, a hooked beak, and sharp talons

owlet – a baby owl

pellet – indigestible bones, feathers, and fur regurgitated by a bird of prey

prey – an animal hunted and killed by another for food

raptor – a bird of prey

talon – sharp, hooked claw or foot belonging to a bird of prey

Where to Learn More about Owls

Some books about owls:

Duncan, James R. *Owls of the World: Their Lives, Behavior, and Survival.* Firefly Books, 2003.

Parry-Jones, Jemima. *Understanding Owls.* United Kingdom: David and Charles, 1998.

Sattler, Helen Roney. *The Book of North American Owls.* Clarion Books, 1998. (ages 9–12)

Waddell, Martin. *Owl Babies.* Candlewick, 2000. (ages 4–8)

Some good owl websites:

www.owlpages.com

www.owling.com

www.owls.org

About the Author

Laura Wyatt is Curator of Wildlife at Flamingo Gardens in Davie, Florida. One of her specialties there is falconry. She is a caretaker of permanently injured, endangered, and nonreleasable Florida native wildlife. She provides these animals with naturalistic habitats and proper care, and pairs them with mates. They will then produce healthy offspring that are trained and released to the wild. Laura has raised and released more than 1,000 Florida native animals, including owls, hawks, river otters, and a large collection of wading birds and waterfowl.

Index

Photographs are indicated by boldface type.

Here are all of the books in this series. Written for children aged 6–9, each book has 20 questions and answers, 20 photos, and 20 funny illustrations by Steve Weaver. For a complete catalog, visit our website at www.pineapplepress.com.

Those Amazing Alligators by Kathy Feeney. Discover the differences between alligators and crocodiles. Learn what alligators eat, how they communicate, and much more.

Those Beautiful Butterflies by Sarah Cussen. Learn all about butterflies—their behavior, why they look the way they do, how they communicate, and why they love bright flowers.

Those Big Bears by Jan Lee Wicker. Why do bears stand on two legs? How do they use their claws? How many kinds are there? What do they do all winter?

Those Colossal Cats by Marta Magellan. Meet lions, tigers, leopards, and the other big cats. Do they purr? How fast can they run? Which is biggest?

Those Delightful Dolphins by Jan Lee Wicker. Dolphins are delightful in the way they communicate and play with one another and the way they cooperate with humans.

Those Enormous Elephants by Sarah Cussen. What is the main function of an elephant's trunk: a straw, a nose, or a hand? If you guessed all three, you're right! Discover more fascinating facts about the largest land animal on earth.

Those Excellent Eagles by Jan Lee Wicker. Learn all about those excellent eagles—what they eat, how fast they fly, why the American bald eagle is our nation's national bird.

Those Funny Flamingos by Jan Lee Wicker. Why are these funny birds pink? Why do they stand on one leg and eat upside down? Where do they live?

Those Kooky Kangaroos by Bonnie Nickel. Why are kangaroos called boomers, fliers, and stinkers? Do they live in trees? Why do they have built-in air conditioning?

Those Lively Lizards by Marta Magellan. Meet lizards that can run on water, some with funny-looking eyes, some that change color, and some that look like little dinosaurs.

Those Magical Manatees by Jan Lee Wicker. Why are they magical? How big are they? What do they eat? Why are they endangered and what can you do to help?

Those Mischievous Monkeys by Bonnie Nickel. Find out where in the world monkeys live, what they eat, and what they do for fun.

Those Outrageous Owls by Laura Wyatt. Learn what owls eat, how they hunt, and why they look the way they do. How do they fly so quietly? Why do horned owls have horns?

Those Peculiar Pelicans by Sarah Cussen. Find out how much food those peculiar pelicans can fit in their beaks, how they stay cool, and whether they really steal fish from fishermen.

Those Perky Penguins by Sarah Cussen. Can penguins fly? Do they get cold? How many kinds are there and where in the world do they live?

Those Terrific Turtles by Sarah Cussen. You'll learn the difference between a turtle and a tortoise, and find out why they have shells. Meet baby turtles and some very, very old ones.

Those Voracious Vultures by Marta Magellan. Learn all about vultures—the gross things they do, what they eat, whether a turkey vulture gobbles, and more.

CPSIA information can be obtained at www.ICGtesting.com
Printed in the USA
BVOW10s0029051213

338212BV00002BA/2/P